BATHROOM SPORTS COMPANION

—— • ——

by

Jack Kreismer

RED-LETTER PRESS, INC.
Saddle River, New Jersey

THE BATHROOM SPORTS COMPANION
COPYRIGHT ©2015 Red-Letter Press, Inc.
ISBN-13: 978-1-60387-096-2
ISBN: 1-60387-096-2

All Rights Reserved
Printed in the United States of America

Red-Letter Press, Inc.
P.O. Box 393
Saddle River, NJ 07458

www.Red-LetterPress.com

ACKNOWLEDGMENTS

BOOK DESIGN & TYPOGRAPHY:
Jeff Kreismer

•

COVER ART:
Jeff Godby

•

RESEARCH & DEVELOPMENT:
Sparky Benjamin

The BATHROOM SPORTS COMPANION

First Quarter

Q&A

First of All

1. Who comes first, alphabetically, in the Pro Basketball Hall of Fame?

2. Who was the first play-by-play announcer for *Monday Night Football*?

3. Who was the first major leaguer to hit 70 home runs in a single season?

4. Who was the first female referee in the NFL?

5. Who was the first freshman to win the Heisman Trophy?

> They've (the Baseball Hall of Fame) got a broadcasters' wing and a players' wing. Maybe one day they'll have a chicken wing.
> *-Ted Giannoulas, a.k.a. "Chicken," the mascot*

That is really a lovely horse.
I once rode her mother.

-Ted Walsh, horse racing commentator

Grab Bag

6. A major league starting pitcher must work at least how many innings to get credit for a victory?
a) 5   b) 6   c) 7

7. The 11th, 12th, and 13th holes at Augusta National are traditionally called what?

8. In 2014, what San Francisco Giants pitcher hurled his second no-hitter in less than a year against the San Diego Padres?

Until 2009, port-a-potties in the infield of the Preakness race course were lined up in long rows. At the same time, patrons were allowed to bring their own alcohol into the event, creating one of the most infamous traditions in the history of day drinking- the running (on top) of the toilets. What race track hosts the Preakness?

Pimlico

9. Which has the most teams: the NFL, NBA, NHL or MLB?

10. What player has won the most World Series rings?

Fact or Flush?

11. One of Floyd Mayweather Jr.'s fight managers during his amateur ring days was a woman, Karina Smirnoff.

12. Wilt Chamberlain never fouled out of an NBA game.

13. Famed for his broken bat home run, Bo Jackson became known as The Splendid Splinter.

14. Stephen Curry wears number 30 as a tribute to his father, Dell, who also wore that number during his NBA career.

Exactly how intricate a sport is jogging? You were two years old; you ran after the cat; you pretty much had it mastered.

-Rick Reilly

> I don't think there's anybody in this organization not focused on the 49ers... I mean Chargers.
>
> *-Bill Belichick, on his team's preparation*

15. The Dallas Cowboys were originally called the Steers.

16. Woody Johnson, the owner of the New York Jets, is part of the Johnson & Johnson family, makers of Band-Aids.

17. Jordan Spieth's winnings at the 2015 Masters were more than Arnold Palmer made during his entire PGA career.

18. The NHL champion Boston Bruins name is spelled BQSTQN BRUINS on the Stanley Cup for their 1971-72 title.

Grab Bag

19. Of the superstar tennis sisters, which is older: Serena or Venus Williams?

20. How many consecutive strikes are needed in bowling for a turkey?

21. The first team name to be retired in NFL history occurred in 1998. What team?

22. This boxer handed Muhammad Ali his first professional defeat in 1971.

23. True or false? Pele was never the leading scorer in a World Cup series.

24. What former U.S. president played college baseball at Yale University?

25. This National High School quarterback of the year in 2000 turned down a Florida State football scholarship to play big league baseball.

Stadia-Mania

26. Until 1988, what Major League Baseball stadium did not have lights?

27. Where is tennis' U.S. Open annually played?

Why should we have to go to class if we came here to play football, we ain't come to play school, classes are pointless.

-Tweet by Ohio State quarterback Cardale Jones

I go bowling every four years
to make sure I still hate it.
-Charlie Ward

28. What current facility houses two NBA teams and one NHL club simultaneously?

29. In 2014, for the first time ever, Super Bowl XLVIII was held in an outdoor venue in a cold weather environment. Where was it played?

30. Centennial Olympic Stadium, the main venue for the 1996 Summer Olympics, was reconfigured to become the new home of what MLB team?

Grab Bag

31. Who's the model for the NBA's silhouette logo?

32. What was the original nickname of the New York Jets?

33. If a baseball player has earned the golden sombrero, what has he done?

34. Name the host city of the 2016 Summer Olympics.

35. What does ESPN stand for?

36. Wayne Gretzky is the NHL's all-time leading scorer. Who's second?

37. Who is the only player in MLB history to win back-to-back All-Star Game MVP Awards?

38. What baseball stadium began the tradition of the "Sausage Race"?

39. How long is a tennis court?

a) 58'   b) 68'   c) 78'   d) 88'

40. How many NBA team nicknames do not end in the letter "s"?

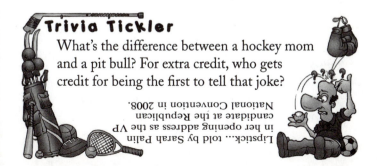

Trivia Tickler

What's the difference between a hockey mom and a pit bull? For extra credit, who gets credit for being the first to tell that joke?

Lipstick… told by Sarah Palin in her opening address as the VP candidate at the Republican National Convention in 2008.

> If you're not into sports, guys
> think you're less of a man unless you can account
> for time in activities equally masculine. When they ask,
> "Wanna go see the game?" I reply, "I can't. I gotta
> go put a transmission in the stripper's car."
>
> *-Bob Nickman*

The Triple Crown

41. In order, what are the three legs of horse racing's Triple Crown?

42. Which race is known as the Test of the Champion?

43. American Pharaoh won the Triple Crown in 2015, ending a 37-year drought. Who, in 1978, was the last winner?

44. What horse set records in all three Triple Crown events in 1973, records that still stand today?

45. He's the only jockey to win the Triple Crown twice, with Whirlaway in 1941 and Citation in 1948. Name him.

46. Who are the only two pro golfers to win three championships in the same year?

47. In 2012, who became the most recent player to win baseball's Triple Crown?

48. What baseball player was a Triple Crown winner in 1942 and 1947 yet was denied the MVP award both years?

49. In 1934, who became a Triple Crown winner for the second consecutive year and then became the first athlete to appear on a box of Wheaties?

50. True or false? No National Leaguer has won the Triple Crown in more than 75 years.

They broke it to me gently. The manager came up to me and told me they didn't allow visitors in the clubhouse.

-Baseball broadcaster Bob Uecker, on being cut during his playing days

> I believe that professional wrestling is real and everything else in the world is fixed.
> *-Sportswriter Frank DeFord*

Answers

1. Kareem Abdul-Jabbar

2. Keith Jackson

3. Mark McGwire, in 1998

4. Sarah Thomas, in 2015

5. Johnny Manziel, in 2012

6. a) 5

7. Amen Corner

8. Tim Lincecum

9. The NFL, 32 (The others have 30.)

San Antonio Spurs point guard Tony Parker was raised in the land once ruled by King Francis I, who purchased the Mona Lisa in 1517 to hang in the bathroom. Name this country.

France

10. Yogi Berra, who won 10 World Series in 14 postseasons with the Yankees

11. Flush- Smirnoff was Mayweather's dance partner on Season 5 of ABC-TV's *Dancing with the Stars*.

12. Fact

13. Flush- Teddy Ballgame aka Ted Williams was aka The Splendid Splinter.

14. Fact

15. Fact

16. Fact

17. Flush- Not by much, though. Spieth took home the green jacket and $1.8 million. Palmer made $1,861,857 in 734 PGA Tour career starts over 53 years.

18. Fact

19. Venus, by a year

20. Three

One of my favorite Olympic events is the luge. This is on the bobsled run, but there's no sled. It's just Bob. It's just a human being hanging on for dear life.

-Jerry Seinfeld

> I went through baseball as a player
> to be named later.
> -*Joe Garagiola*

21. The Oilers- When the Tennessee Oilers (nee Houston) decided to change their name to the Titans, the NFL decided to retire the former name.

22. Joe Frazier

23. True

24. George H.W. Bush

25. Joe Mauer

26. Chicago's Wrigley Field

27. Arthur Ashe Stadium, in Flushing, NY

28. L.A.'s Staples Center, home to the Lakers, Clippers and Kings

29. MetLife Stadium in East Rutherford, NJ

30. Atlanta Braves (It became Turner Field. The Braves will be on the move again in 2017, to SunTrust Park in nearby Cobb County.)

31. Jerry West

32. Titans

33. He has struck out four times in one game.

34. Rio de Janeiro

35. Entertainment Sports Programming Network

36. Mark Messier (Gretzky scored 2,857 points, Messier 1,887.)

37. Mike Trout, in 2014 and '15

38. County Stadium in Milwaukee - The tradition continued when the Brewers moved into Miller Park in 2001.

39. c) 78 feet

40. Four - Miami Heat, Oklahoma City Thunder, Orlando Magic, and Utah Jazz

41. The Kentucky Derby, the Preakness, and the Belmont

42. The Belmont

43. Affirmed

44. Secretariat

45. Eddie Arcaro

You hear about how many fourth quarter comebacks that a guy has and I think it means a guy screwed up in the first three quarters.

-Peyton Manning

We tried everything. We played four
white guys and an Egyptian.

-Louisville Cardinals basketball coach Rick Pitino,
responding to accusations that he was
running up the score

46. Ben Hogan, 1953 and Tiger Woods, 2000

47. Miguel Cabrera

48. Ted Williams (Joe Gordon and Joe DiMaggio
were the respective winners.)

49. Lou Gehrig

50. True- Joe Medwick was the last Triple Crown
winner in the NL, in 1937.

Second Quarter

Facts & Fancies

We Can't Make This Stuff Up...

In 2007, Gabe Gross of the Milwaukee Brewers was thrown out at third after manager Ned Yost's scratch of a mosquito bite was misinterpreted for a steal sign... Former horse racing Triple Crown winner Affirmed once got loose at Hollywood Park, prompting a trackwide search. The missing horse was located back in his own stall - which he had found among 2,244 others... In 1916, Cumberland College suffered the worst football defeat in college history, 222-0...

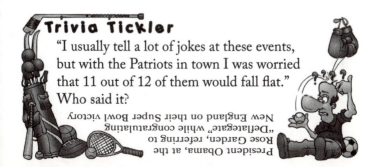

Trivia Tickler

"I usually tell a lot of jokes at these events, but with the Patriots in town I was worried that 11 out of 12 of them would fall flat." Who said it?

President Obama, at the Rose Garden, referring to "Deflategate" while congratulating New England on their Super Bowl victory

That picture was taken out of context.

-Jeff Innis, New York Mets pitcher,
on an unflattering photo of him

Jack Dempsey bought a Rolls-Royce after each successful heavyweight title fight - six in all... A member of Tokyo's 2016 Olympic bid committee, fearing the perils of global warming, warned that, "It could be that the 2016 Games are the last Olympics in the history of mankind." (P.S. Tokyo didn't win the bid.) ... The 1898 Boston Marathon was won by Ronald McDonald.

Rerun Rampage

24-year-old Bryan Allison suffered multiple injuries in 2001 when he fell to the ground while throwing a 25-inch TV set off the second-floor porch of his home in Niagara Falls, N.Y, after watching a video of a 1989 hockey playoff game. He and his brother tossed the TV when they became upset over the outcome, which was presumably the same result as twelve years earlier.

A Madagascar soccer team, protesting what they thought was biased refereeing, spent an entire match scoring own goals on themselves. The game ended 149-0.

•

Until 1937, a jump ball in basketball took place at center court after every single made basket.

•

Tug-of-war was an Olympic sport from 1900-1920.

•

According to the *Wall Street Journal*, the actual playing time of a Major League Baseball game is under 18 minutes.

•

An NFL Players Association study concluded that the average player's career is 3.3 years. Punters have the most longevity, an average of 4.87 years, while a running back's career is the shortest, 2.57.

People say, "Since you got rich and famous, you've become insufferable." I say, That's not true. I've always been insufferable.

-Shannon Sharpe

Interest your kids in bowling.
Get them off the streets and into the alleys.
-Don Rickles

Court Jesters

On being misquoted in his own autobiography, Hall of Famer Charles Barkley said, "I should have read it."

•••

Bill Russell had an impersonator who was almost a dead ringer for the Basketball Hall of Famer exeept for one thing: he was nine inches shorter than the 6'9" Celtics former center. The Russell wannabe got around this by claiming he had shortening surgery so he could fit into his Mercedes.

This college team has won two NCAA baseball championships and has seen several players go on to the majors, including Yankees outfielder Jacoby Ellsbury. Hint: The team nickname is partially contained in the title of the first TV program to ever show a a toilet on screen.

Oregon State Beavers-
Leave it to Beaver is the television show.

With an NBA lockout looming, Deron Williams signed with the Turkish Basketball League during the 2011 offseason. While his time there was short, he clearly made an impression. His Besiktas team retired his #8 jersey after only 15 games.

•••

In a 1974 contest, Lakers center Elmore Smith stood at the foul line with three shots ahead of him. He needed to make only two to keep the game going. Not only did Smith miss all three- on each one of his shots he came up with nothing but air.

There Is No Joy In Friendsville

From 1967 to 1973, Tennessee's Friendsville Academy high school basketball team chalked up a national record 138 consecutive losses. They lost one game 71 to 0 but another only 2 to 0 when the winning basket was scored by a

I wanted to have a career in sports when I was young, but I had to give it up. I'm only six feet tall, so I couldn't play basketball. I'm only 190 pounds, so I couldn't play football. And I have 20-20 vision, so I couldn't be a referee.

-Jay Leno

> Lennox Lewis, I'm coming for you, man…
> I want your heart. I want to eat his children.
> Praise be to Allah!
> *-Mike Tyson*

Friendsville player, who shot the ball into the wrong hoop.

In 1970, the coach named one player--a player who had never scored a single point--the team's MVP. When reporter Douglas S. Looney from the *National Observer* questioned the coach, he tersely replied, "You don't think scoring is everything, do you?"

The conversation continued with the reporter asking, "Is there anything this team does well?"

"Not really," replied the coach.

"Are you making progress?"

"I couldn't truthfully say that we are."

"Do you like coaching?"

"I don't care that much for basketball."

Bird's the Word

While it's not all that unusual for a baseball card to be printed with an error, there was one instance in particular in which the manufacturer was understandably embarrassed.

The card was a 1989 Fleer Billy Ripken. Pictured in his Baltimore Orioles uniform, Ripken's bat was perched over his right shoulder with the bottom of the knob visible. The original version was printed with an expletive that had been written on the knob.

When the error was found, Fleer rushed to correct it, resulting in variations of the card being covered with marker, brushed with whiteout, and airbrushed.

Needless to say, the uncensored card remains the most sought after version.

This team is one execution away from being a very good basketball team.
-Doc Rivers

> The Mets have gotten their leadoff batter
> on base only once this inning.
> *-Broadcaster Ralph Kiner*

Hall of Fame catcher Johnny Bench could hold seven baseballs in one hand.

•

Movie legend Clint Eastwood saved the life of tournament director Steve John at the 2014 Pebble Beach National Pro-Am when John choked on a piece of cheese and Eastwood performed the Heimlich maneuver.

•

The New York Islanders, who now play in Brooklyn, offered fans .5 ounce vials of "melted ice" from their final home game at Nassau Coliseum, where they'd skated for 43 years. The collectible went for $20 a bottle and sold out in three hours.

•

Former President George W. Bush and his future wife Laura spent their first date at a miniature golf course.

There are 575 words in the epic poem *Casey at the Bat*.

•

There are 1,661,220 inches in a marathon.

What's in a Name?

• A racecar driver was fined $30,000 for losing his composure and making an obscene gesture. His name? Will Power.

• In 2011, the St. John's Red Storm recruited the son of a Nigerian minister to play on their basketball team. His name? God's Gift Achiuwa. His brother's name? God's Will.

• When 7'2" Dikembe Mutombo, a four-time NBA Defensive Player of the Year, was born in Zaire on June 25, 1966, he was named Dikembe Mutombo Mpolondo Mukamba Jean-Jacque Wamutombo.

Trivia Tickler

When questioned about making more money than President Herbert Hoover in 1930, what ballplayer said, "I had a better year than he did"?

Babe Ruth

How would you like a job where every time you make a mistake, a big red light goes on and 18,000 people boo?

-Hall of Fame goalie Jacques Plante

Hot Corner Potato

In a 1980s minor league baseball game, Williamsport hosted Reading. With an act that could've been drawn up in the schoolyard, perhaps it was fitting that the game's memorable moment occurred in the same city as the Little League World Series.

With a Reading runner on third, Williamsport catcher Dave Bresnahan had a trick up his sleeve. Actually, it was in his catcher's mitt. There, Bresnahan kept a potato hidden.

After a pitch, he grabbed the potato and purposely threw it wildly toward third base. The runner, believing it was the baseball, trotted home. When he arrived there, Bresnahan greeted him with the baseball he was still holding.

The umpire, not amused, called the runner safe. Neither were Bresnahan's bosses. The next day, he was let go.

Aaron Rodgers took in $50,000 for his charity when he won a celebrity *Jeopardy!* game over his opponents, *Shark Tank's* Kevin O'Leary and astronaut Mark Kelly, in 2015.

•

The symbol "K," used to signify a strikeout in baseball, comes from the word "struck."

•

As the coach of the Super Bowl XLIII champion Pittsburgh Steelers, 36-year-old Mike Tomlin was the youngest coach to win a Super Bowl.

•

NY Mets manager Bobby Valentine, ejected from a game in 1999, went into the clubhouse, put on regular clothes and a fake mustache, and then returned to the dugout. He was fined $5,000 by the commissioner for returning after an ejection.

I watched the Indy 500, and I was thinking that if they left earlier they wouldn't have to go so fast.

-*Steven Wright*

> Quit coaching? I'd croak in a week.
>
> *-Bear Bryant, who died of a heart attack*
> *a month after retiring*

Spellbinding

• The Minnesota Timberwolves handed out posters with their nickname spelled W-O-V-E-S on "Reading to Succeed Night" at the Target Center in Minneapolis.

• In 1960, the Chicago White Sox became the first big league team to put player names on the backs of uniforms- and also the first to do so incorrectly. On a road trip to New York, the back of first baseman Ted Kluszewski's jersey featured a backwards "z" and an "x" instead of "k" in his name.

Walter Alcock invented perforated toilet paper in 1879. He happens to have the same initials as a Hall of Fame baseball manager who signed 23 one-year contracts with the Dodgers. Who is he?

Walter Alston

• During a World Series broadcast, network commentator Tim McCarver proclaimed, "It's a five-letter word- S-T-R-I-K-E."

• An Ohio State online photo gallery depicted Buckeyes fans spelling out O-H-I-O with their bodies. It featured a shot in which the corpse of a man in a coffin played the role of the I.

• In a game against the Marlins in 2009, Adam Dunn and Ryan Zimmerman, two of the top hitters on the Washington Nationals, were sent onto the field wearing "Natinals" jerseys.

Knock Yourself Out

Boxer Daniel Caruso was getting psyched for a 1992 Golden Gloves bout in New York, pounding his gloves into his face just before the bell rang. He accidentally rang his own bell. Caruso punched himself in the nose, bloodying and breaking it. Doctors stopped the bout before it began.

A virgin.

-Rory McIlroy, when asked what he would be if he hadn't taken up golf

I didn't make this decision by myself.
Thirty teams helped me make it.
*-Garret Anderson, former Angels outfielder,
on retiring*

Major League Mishaps

• Adam Eaton stabbed himself in the stomach as
he was using a knife to open a DVD wrapper.

• Bret Barberie missed a game because he
mistakenly rubbed chili juice in his eyes.

• Ken Griffey, Jr. was forced to miss a game after
his cup slipped and pinched a testicle.

• Marty Cordova fell asleep in a tanning bed,
badly burning himself. He was forced to stay out
of direct sunlight, which meant missing several
day games.

• After having a nightmare about spiders,
Glenallen Hill fell out of bed onto a glass table,
receiving cuts over much of his body.

• John Smoltz burned his chest while trying to
iron the shirt he was wearing.

Halftime Humor

A Boston marathoner suffered a sudden spell of dizziness so he stopped for a minute and rested his head between his legs.

Seeing this, a preppy Harvard student asked in very proper fashion, "Have you vertigo?"

The marathoner said, "Yes. Four more miles."

Then there was the dentist who complimented the hockey player on his nice, even teeth: one, three, five, seven and nine were missing.

> The three toughest fighters I've ever been up against were Sugar Ray Robinson, Sugar Ray Robinson, and Sugar Ray Robinson. I fought Sugar so many times, I'm surprised I'm not diabetic!
> -Jake LaMotta

> **When Sandy Koufax retired.**
> *-Willie Stargell, on his greatest thrill in baseball*

Q: Why were the 76ers the last NBA team to get a website?

A: Because they couldn't put up three W's in a row.

Boulderdash University decides to field a rowing team. Alas, inexperience breeds defeat and they lose race after race. Tired of being the league's doormat, B.U. sends team captain Chuckie Limburger to spy on Harvard, the perennial powerhouse.

Chuckie hides in the bushes along the Charles River in Cambridge and watches the Harvard team practice for a week. When he returns to B.U., he announces to his teammates that he's figured out their secret. "What is it?" one of them shouts out.

"We should have only one guy yelling. The other eight should row."

A sports nut was strolling along the Cleveland shores of Lake Erie when he spotted a bottle floating in the water. As it drifted ashore, he picked it up and out popped a Genie.

"Master, Master," said the Genie, "I am eternally grateful that you have released me from my bondage in this bottle. It has been ages since I've experienced freedom. For your reward, ask any three wishes and I will grant them to you."

The guy thought for a moment and said, "I would like for three things to happen this year- for the Indians to win the World Series, the Cavs to win the NBA title, and the Browns to win the Super Bowl."

The Genie pondered this for a second- and then jumped back in the bottle.

Trivia Tickler

The funniest home run in baseball history occurred in 1993 when Carmelo Martinez of the Indians hit a ball which went over the fence after bouncing off the head of what Rangers right fielder?

Jose Canseco

> Hockey players wear numbers
> because you can't always identify the
> body with dental records.
> -Bob Plager

A guy comes home from work, plops himself onto his Barcolounger in the family room, grabs the remote, and flips on the football game on the big screen HDTV. He yells into the kitchen, "Honey, bring me a cold one before it starts."

His wife brings him a chilled mug of beer. A few minutes later, he calls out to the wife again, "Honey, bring me another beer before it starts."

Again, his wife brings him a beer. A short time later, he yells a third time, "Honey, hurry up and bring me another beer before it starts."

The wife, now exasperated, marches into the family room and says, "You bum. I've been doing the wash... the dishes... the ironing... and now I'm waiting on you hand and foot!"

As she reads him the riot act, the husband rolls his eyes and sighs quietly, "Oh no, it's started already."

Usain Bolt was about to enter an upscale club when a bouncer stopped him. "You can't come in here wearing jeans," he said.

"Don't you know who I am?" said the world's fastest human.

"Of course I do," replied the bouncer. "And it won't take you long to run home and get changed."

At the summer Olympic Games, a girl bumped into a guy carrying an eight-foot long stick.

"Excuse me," said the girl, "but are you by any chance a pole vaulter?"

"Nein, I'm a German, but how did you know my name is Valter?"

If the Cincinnati Reds were really the first major league baseball team, who did they play?
-George Carlin

> I should be a postage stamp.
> That's the only way I'll ever be licked.
> *-Muhammad Ali*

A guy walks into a sports bar with his German Shepherd. He asks the bartender for a beer. The bartender looks down and says, "I'm sorry, we don't allow dogs here."

The fellow thinks quickly and responds, "He's my seeing-eye dog."

"Oh, I'm sorry," says the bartender. "Here, have one on the house." He pours the guy a beer.

The guy thanks the bartender for the beer, settles down at a table near the door, and begins to watch the football game on the nearest HDTV.

The toilet is sometimes referred to as the Oval Office, remindful of the presidency and the first chief executive to throw out the ceremonial first pitch on baseball's Opening Day. The year was 1910. Name the president.

William Howard Taft, who threw out the ball at Griffith Stadium in Washington, D.C., preceding a Senators-Philadelphia A's game

Pretty soon, another guy comes walking in with a small dog. The guy with the German Shepherd whispers, "Psst, buddy. Lemme give you a little tip. They don't allow dogs in here. You gotta tell the bartender that you have a seeing-eye dog."

The other fellow with the pooch thanks him and moseys on up to the bar. "I'll have a draft," he says to the bartender.

The bartender says, "I'm sorry, we don't allow dogs."

The guy answers, "But I'm blind and this is my seeing-eye dog."

The bartender says, "I don't think so. That's a Chihuahua."

The guy says, "What... They gave me a Chihuahua!?!"

Jack Del Rio and myself are very similar except he's really good looking and was a great player. Other than that we're very similar.

-Buffalo Bills coach Rex Ryan

> When we lost, I couldn't sleep all night. When we win, I can't sleep at night. But when you win, you wake up feeling better.
>
> -Joe Torre

A priest, a doctor and a lawyer were becoming frustrated with the slow play of the foursome ahead of them. "What's with these guys?" the lawyer grumbled. "We've been waiting to tee off at least 15 minutes."

"Here comes the greenskeeper," said the priest. "Let's have a word with him."

When confronted, the greenskeeper advised them that the slow-playing group were firefighters and that, sadly, they all lost their sight while saving the clubhouse from a fire a year ago. In gratitude, the club allowed them to play for free anytime.

The priest expressed his concern and said he'd keep them in his prayers, while the doctor volunteered to contact an ophthalmologist buddy to see if there was anything he could do for them.

The lawyer said, "Why can't these guys play at night?"

At a hoity-toity country club where rules of golf are strictly enforced, a member saw that a guest of the club had his ball five inches in front of the tee markers. The member hurriedly went over to the guest and said, "Sir, I don't know whether you've ever played here before, but we have very stringent rules about placing your tee at or behind the markers before driving the ball."

The guest looked the snooty club member right in the eye and retorted, "First, I've never played here before. Second, I don't care about your rules. And third, this is my second shot."

Q: What do you get when you cross an evil woman with a Sandy Koufax curveball?

A: The wicked pitch of the west.

I used to play sports. Then I realized you can buy trophies. Now I'm good at everything.

-Demetri Martin

By the age of 18, the average American has witnessed 200,000 acts of violence on television, most of them occurring during Game 1 of the NHL playoff series.

-Sportswriter Steve Rushin

Maybe you've heard about the jockey who was a tremendous overeater. He kept putting a la carte before the horse.

Then there was the horse that came in so late the jockey was wearing pajamas.

Q: How are judges and basketball refs alike?

A: They both work the courts.

Third Quarter

Q&A

Playing By The Rules

1. According to new NFL rules adopted in 2015, the ball is placed on what yard line for the extra point kick?

2. How many technical fouls result in ejection from an NBA game?

3. In tennis, your serve goes wild and hits the recipient on the fly. Do you get credit for the point?

Trivia Tickler

What former NFL head coach was featured in a humorous beer commercial ranting, "Playoffs!? You kiddin' me? Playoffs!? Don't talk about playoffs!"?

Jim Mora

> One loss is good for the soul.
> Too many losses are not good for the coach.
> *-Knute Rockne*

4. The first baseman trips and loses his glove. As he is lying on his stomach, he reaches out and makes the catch in his hat. Is this a legal catch?

5. A defensive player bats a forward pass up in the air. The quarterback catches his own pass. May he throw another forward pass?

6. What's the minimum number of players an NBA team must make available, meaning dressed in uniform and on the bench, for a game?

7. A field goal attempt grazes the helmet of the offensive right guard before it clears the uprights. Does it count?

8. What is the score of a forfeited NFL game?

9. A line drive hits the pitcher's mound and ricochets into the first base dugout. Place the batter on the correct base.

10. When inbounding a basketball, how much time do you have to release it?

Fore! Play

11. President Bill Clinton was at what golfer's house when he fell down the steps and injured his knee in 1997?

12. How old do you have to be to play on the Champions PGA Tour?

13. What trophy is awarded to the golfer maintaining the lowest scoring average in PGA events?

14. At 5'4" tall, he is the shortest winner of The Masters. Name him. (Hint: His Masters victory came in 1991.)

15. Jordan Spieth won the 2015 Masters as he led wire-to-wire and shot a record-tying 270 to win his first major at the age of 21. He finished four strokes ahead of two runners-up. Can you name either of them?

> If you come in second,
> you're just the first loser.
> *-Tiger Woods*

> A lot of guys who have never choked,
> have never been in position to do so.
> *-Golfer Tom Watson*

Grab Bag

16. The world's fastest man ever, Usain Bolt, hails from what country?

17. In 1962, the Cleveland Indians traded Harry Chiti to the New York Mets for a player to be named later. Who became that player?

18. Name the only team to make a Super Bowl appearance in each of the last five decades (including this one). Hint: It's also the only NFL team that has a logo on just one side of its helmet.

Bathroom chaos occurred at what legendary stadium on Opening Night, April 5, 2015, as there were only two facilities open on the main concourse and none in the upper deck due to ongoing renovations?

Wrigley Field- Portable potties were installed the next day.

19. Who's the all-time winningest coach in college basketball history, either men's or women's?

20. Two brothers, Pete and Jerry Cusimano, began a tradition by throwing what onto the Detroit Red Wings home ice in 1952?

21. Who was the last player to wear #42 after Jackie Robinson's number was retired by Major League Baseball?

By The Numbers

22. The Cleveland Indians retired the number 455. Why?

23. "The Big E" played exactly 50,000 minutes in his NBA career. Do you know him?

24. Six Pro Football Hall of Fame quarterbacks have worn the #12. How many can you come up with?

How come women don't play ice hockey? Millions of girls played field hockey, and God knows women can skate. Maybe it's the teeth. Women have this vain silly feeling thing about losing their front teeth.

-*Danny Liebert*

> The depressing thing about tennis is that no matter how much I play, I'll never be as good as a wall. I played a wall once. They're relentless.
>
> *-Mitch Hedberg*

25. What NFL team has retired the #12 in honor of their fans, "The 12th Man"?

26. Which NBA great has never worn the #23 during his career: Michael Jordan, Kobe Bryant or LeBron James?

27. The number 2,632 represents what historic baseball figure?

28. In 2007, what baseball team became the first franchise in major professional sports to lose 10,000 games?

29. What long-standing NFL team, which has yet to officially retire any jersey numbers, was the first to display player numbers on the sides of their uniform pants?

30. In 2005, what #92 became the first player in NFL history to have his number officially retired by two teams?

Who Am I?

31. I hold baseball's career stolen base record.

32. I owned the Clippers NBA franchise before Steve Ballmer.

33. I was the last man to defeat Muhammad Ali.

34. I've won the MVP award more times than any other athlete in the four major North American sports leagues (MLB, NBA, NFL, and NHL).

35. I am the longest-tenured broadcaster with the same team in professional sports history.

36. I was the 34th President of the United States and was inducted into the World Golf Hall of Fame in 2009.

37. I played center at UCLA immediately after Kareem and right before Bill Walton. My teams won three NCAA titles.

The most favorite activity of nudists: volleyball.
The least favorite: dodgeball.

-Jay Leno

Why doesn't the fattest man in the world become a hockey goalie?
-*Comedian Steven Wright*

38. I have been on the cover of *Sports Illustrated* more than any other person.

39. With the Indians, I became the first player in MLB history to homer from each side of the plate in the same inning in 1993.

40. I won the Cy Young Award four years in a row (1992-95) and became a baseball Hall of Famer in 2014.

Grab Bag

41. Including the postseason, what NFL team finished their 1972 season 17-0?

42. The San Antonio Spurs were formerly known as what ABA team?

43. This team won the 2015 Stanley Cup, their first championship at home since 1938.

44. What stadium has been host to the Super Bowl the most times?

Either/Or

45. Who is taller: current Seahawks quarterback Russell Wilson or former QB Doug Flutie?

46. Which women's soccer team has won the most World Cup titles: the United States or Germany?

47. Who was the first fighter to defeat Mike Tyson: Evander Holyfield or Buster Douglas?

48. Who was the last player to win back-to-back MVP Awards: Barry Bonds or Miguel Cabrera?

49. Did either Ernie Banks or Don Mattingly ever play in a World Series?

50. Who was the oldest NFL player: George Blanda or Jerry Rice?

Trivia Tickler

Name the two sibling sports figures who have hosted *Saturday Night Live*.

Peyton and Eli Manning

> I was going so bad that last week I skipped dinner two days because I was down to .198 and I didn't want anyone saying I wasn't hitting my weight.
>
> *-Jesse Barfield, former Blue Jays outfielder*

Answers

1. The fifteen yard line

2. Two

3. Yes

4. No – It's a three base penalty for illegal use of equipment.

5. No

6. Eight

7. No

8. 2-0

9. It's a foul ball.

10. Five seconds

11. Greg Norman

12. 50

13. The Vardon Trophy

14. Ian Woosnam

15. Phil Mickelson and Justin Rose

16. Jamaica

17. Harry Chiti- the only player to ever be traded for himself

18. The Pittsburgh Steelers

19. Pat Summitt

20. An octopus

21. Mariano Rivera

22. It was done symbolically, to represent the number of consecutive sellouts from June 12, 1995 to April 2, 2001.

23. Elvin Hayes

24. Terry Bradshaw, Bob Griese, Arnie Herber, Jim Kelly, Joe Namath and Roger Staubach

25. Seattle Seahawks

26. Kobe Bryant

27. The amount of consecutive games played by Cal Ripken, Jr.

They both wear number 12.

-New England Patriots coach Bill Belichick, when asked to comment on the similarities/differences between quarterbacks Tom Brady and Aaron Rodgers

> You have to give Pete a lot of credit for what he has accomplished. He never went to college, and the only book he ever read was *The Pete Rose Story*.
>
> *-Karolyn Rose, on her ex-husband*

28. Philadelphia Phillies

29. Dallas Cowboys

30. Reggie White, with the Eagles and Packers

31. Rickey Henderson

32. Donald Sterling

33. Trevor Berbick

34. Wayne Gretzky, nine times (eight consecutively)

35. Vin Scully (1950-present)

36. Dwight Eisenhower

37. Steve Patterson

National Bathroom Reading Week occurs the first full week of June (Really!). And it is during the first week of that month- June 3, 1932, to be precise –that this man became the first player to hit four consecutive home runs in one game. Name him.

Lou Gehrig

38. Michael Jordan

39. Carlos Baerga

40. Greg Maddux

41. The Miami Dolphins

42. Dallas Chaparrals

43. Chicago Blackhawks

44. The Mercedez-Benz Superdome in New Orleans, 7

45. Russell Wilson- He's 5'11." Flutie is 5'10."

46. The United States- Since the World Cup was initiated in 1991, the U.S. has won three championships. Germany has taken two World Cup Finals.

47. Buster Douglas

48. Miguel Cabrera, in 2012-13

49. No

50. George Blanda, 48, a kicker and QB for the Raiders in 1975

Were you born that way?
-Jess Rogers, Cubs broadcaster,
while interviewing relief pitcher Antonio Alfonseca,
who has six fingers on each hand

> Its a official dat i am leavin skool and
> enterin draft. ... i aint doin anotha yr.
>
> *-Tommy Mason Griffin, Oklahoma point guard,*
> *declaring his career choice via Facebook*

Teaser Timeout

Baseball Baffler

Nolan Ryan... Bob Feller... Justin Verlander...
Give them their due with their 100 mph heaters,
but they couldn't hold a candle to flame-thrower
Hayden Siddhartha "Sidd" Finch according to
Sports Illustrated's April 1, 1985 cover story.

The magazine reported that the 28-year-old
eccentric rookie from Tibet had been blowing
away the Mets coaching staff during spring
training with far and away the fastest fastball
anyone had ever seen- an amazing 168 miles
per hour.

So why was it, then, that Finch's name made
an equally quick disappearance from the sports
pages?

Note the date of the issue, April 1- It was an April Fool's joke by the publication.

Fourth Quarter

Facts & Fancies

The Blunderful Broadcaster

After his Major League playing career, Jerry Coleman became even more well-known for his malaprops as the longtime play-by-play man of the Padres. The beloved broadcaster passed away in 2014, but here we get to re-live some of his "finest" work.

• Hi folks, I'm Johnny Grubb. No I'm not. This is Jerry Coleman.

• The new Haitian baseball can't weigh more than four ounces or less than five.

High sticking, tripping, slashing, spearing, charging, hooking, fighting, unsportsmanlike conduct, interference, roughing... everything else is just figure skating.

-Scotty Bowman, on the NHL

> Soccer is not a sport
> because you can't use your arms.
> Anything where you can't use your arms
> can't be a sport. Tap dancing isn't a sport.
> I rest my case.
> *-George Carlin*

• He (Graig Nettles) leaped up to make one of those diving stops only he can make.

• Ozzie Smith just made another play that I've never seen anyone else make before, and I've seen him make it more than anyone else ever has.

• Winfield goes back to the wall, he hits his head on the wall and it rolls off! It's rolling all the way back to second base. This is a terrible thing for the Padres.

• And Kansas City is at Chicago tonight, or is that Chicago at Kansas City? Well, no matter, Kansas City leads in the eighth, four to four.

• Next up is Fernando Gonzalez, who is not playing tonight.

• Rich Folkers is throwing up in the bullpen.

• There's a hard shot to LeMaster, and he throws Madlock into the dugout.

• McCovey swings and misses, and it's fouled back.

• Larry Lintz steals second standing up. He slid, but he didn't have to.

• The ex-left-hander Dave Roberts will be going for Houston.

• Sometimes, big trees grow out of acorns. I think I heard that from a squirrel.

• The Phillies beat the Cubs today in the double-header. That puts another keg in the Cubs' coffin.

• If (Pete) Rose's streak were still intact, with that single to left, the fans would be throwing babies out of the upper deck.

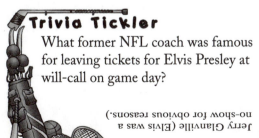

Trivia Tickler

What former NFL coach was famous for leaving tickets for Elvis Presley at will-call on game day?

Jerry Glanville (Elvis was a no-show for obvious reasons.)

> I really don't like talking about money.
> All I can say is that the Good Lord must
> have wanted me to have it.
>
> *-Larry Bird*

Babe Ruth is credited as the first player to order a bat with a knob on it, produced by Louisville Slugger in 1919.

•

The mother of former NBA star Grant Hill was a roommate of Hillary Clinton at Wellesley.

•

In San Diego in 2015, 92-year-old Harriette Thompson became the oldest woman to complete a full 26.2-mile marathon with a time of 7:24:36.

•

Left fielder Carlos May, who played most of his ten-year big league career with the Chicago White Sox, is the only player to wear his birthdate on the back of his uniform. Carlos was born May 17.

•

At a 1990s minor league contest in Durham between the Bulls and Winston-Salem, a brawl broke out and ten players were ejected. It was "Strike Out Domestic Violence Night."

Headers

In 2011, Aaron Eccleston, an amateur soccer player in Australia, was ejected from a match after refs found him in breach of uniform rules for wearing an "intimate body piercing." The infraction was uncovered when a ball struck Eccleston in the groin and he fell in agony to the ground, then pulled down his shorts to check for damage.

•••

Somalia, a midfielder for the Brazilian soccer club Botafogo, was charged with falsely reporting a crime to Rio de Janeiro police after he made up a story about being kidnapped when he was actually trying to avoid a fine for being late to practice.

•••

Aurel Rusu, the president of a Romanian soccer team, was so dismayed by his team's dismal play that he appointed his son Lucian as the new manager in 1997. Lucian was six months old at the time.

> Has anybody every satisfactorily explained why the bad hop is always the last one?
> *-Broadcaster Hank Greenwald*

> If we were looking for citizenship, we'd disband the league.
>
> *-Kevin McHale, when asked how important character is in the NBA Draft*

Pit Stops

A bank robber in Fairview, Pa., who disguised himself with a coat of drywall compound forgot to mask the appearance of the NASCAR-themed Rusty Wallace license plate on his getaway car. Witnesses recognized it and it led ultimately to the conviction of the thief.

•••

A 67-year-old New Jersey man accepted probation, community service and a $1,000 fine after admitting to charges of shooting his family's 20-year-old African Gray parrot with a pellet gun. He said it interrupted his viewing of a televised NASCAR race.

USA Today calls this John Brown University basketball home opener tradition the "best technical foul in all of sports." Thousands of fans come armed with what item and hurl it onto the court after the first field goal by JBU?

A roll of toilet paper- The event is known as the annual Toilet Paper Game.

According to various sources, in 2015, Denver Broncos players began levying a "fart tax" on anyone breaking wind during team meetings. Pro Bowl linebacker Von Miller was said to be particularly unhappy with the price of gas as he was reportedly the biggest offender.

•

North Carolina coaching legend Dean Smith left every single player he coached (from 1961-1997) $200 in his will. Before he died, he arranged for his estate to send a check for that amount in the mail along with the message, "Enjoy a dinner out compliments of Dean Smith."

•

The Triple-A Tacoma Rainiers once held an "Umbrella Night." It was rained out.

•

In 2009, Tiger Woods set a record for appearing or being mentioned on the cover of the *New York Post* for 20 straight days. The coverage had nothing to do with golf.

Always go to other people's funerals, otherwise they won't come to yours.

-*Yogi Berra*

It could permanently hurt a
batter for a long time.
-Pete Rose, on the brushback pitch

Former heavyweight champion Leon Spinks was
once mugged by some thugs who made off with
his money and jewelry- in addition to his two gold
front teeth.

•

The New York Giants and Jets jointly owned
property in the Meadowlands is called MetLife
Stadium but the clubs previously turned down a
naming rights offer of $25 million from
AshleyMadison.com, an online service for
adulterers.

•

When the $23 million Dodger Stadium opened
in 1962, there were no drinking fountains.

•

The Milwaukee Brewers held a Bob Wickman
poster giveaway night on July 29, 2000. The
only problem was that the pitcher had been
traded to the Indians the night before the game.

Much Ado About Nothing

In 2003, the Charleston Riverdogs held a "Nobody Night," when no one was allowed in the stadium until after the 5th inning when the game and the attendance- 0 –became official. Fans gathered outside the minor league stadium and rushed in during the 6th inning to collect foul balls that had landed in empty seats during the first five innings.

Grave News

Donald Trump plans to build a cemetery at his Trump National Golf Club in Bedminster, N.J., adjacent to the 5th hole. It'll be the final resting place for The Donald, his family and any of the club's members who wish to be interred there- for an extra fee, no doubt.

I don't create controversies. They're there long before I open my mouth. I just bring them to your attention.

-Charles Barkley

There's some different laws
out here in Colorado. Pizza business is
pretty good out here, believe it or not, due to
some recent law changes.

*-Peyton Manning, referring to the legalization
of marijuana*

Boomer's Best

A mainstay at ESPN since the network's inception, Chris Berman is well known for his catch phrases and the many nicknames he's given athletes. In no particular order, here are ten of his best.

1. Albert "Winnie The" Pujols
2. Harold "Growing" Baines
3. Todd "Highway to" Helton
4. Miguel "Tejada they come, Tejada they fall"
5. Mike "You're in good hands with" Alstott
6. Carlos "One if by land, two if by sea, three if" Baerga
7. Scott "Supercalifragilisticexpiali" Brosius
8. CC "Splish splash I was taking" Sabathia
9. Bert "Be Home" Blyleven
10. Bernard "Innocent until proven" Gilkey

Sudden Death

Killer Trivia

1. What's the name of the award given to the most outstanding men's and women's college basketball players?

a) John R. Wooden Award
b) James Naismith Award
c) Adolph Rupp Trophy
d) Jimmy Valvano Award

2. The New York Yankees retired uniform #8 in honor of two catchers who wore it. One is Yogi Berra. Who's the other?

a) Bill Dickey
b) Johnny Blanchard
c) Thurman Munson
d) Jorge Posada

Trivia Tickler

Name the two comedians who are in the Baseball Hall of Fame.

Abbott and Costello, for their *Who's on First?* routine

American professional athletes are bilingual;
they speak English and profanity.

-*Gordie Howe*

3. What is the drink du jour of the Kentucky
Derby?

a) Kentucky Bourbon
b) Mint Julep
c) Grasshopper
d) Bloody Mary

4. In 2003, he became the first lefthanded golfer
to win the Masters. Name him.

a) Phil Mickelson
b) Bubba Watson
c) Mike Weir
d) Bob Charles

5. When Barry Bonds hit his record-breaking
73 home runs in 2001, who led the American
League in round trippers with 52?

a) Troy Glaus
b) Manny Ramirez
c) Alex Rodriguez
d) Jose Bautista

6. Dressage, eventing and jumping are the three sports or "disciplines" of what event at the Olympics?

a) Curling
b) Equestrian
c) Gymnastics
d) Fencing

7. His birth name was Walker Smith Jr. His fight name was:

a) Jack Dempsey
b) Joe Louis
c) Sugar Ray Robinson
d) Sugar Ray Leonard

8. At 19 years and 342 days old, who was the youngest player to ever win the Heisman Trophy?

a) Johnny Manziel
b) Jameis Winston
c) Archie Griffin
d) Chris Weinke

It's almost exciting to think about all the room for improvement that we have.

-New York Jets quarterback Geno Smith

> I haven't read a book since ninth grade when they made me. (It was) "A Mocking to Remember" or whatever? "A Mockingbird to Remember," I think that was the last book I read.
>
> *-Rob Gronkowski*

9. In 2013, the Cleveland Cavaliers selected Anthony Bennett, making him the first player born in what country to be taken #1 overall in the NBA Draft?

a) Canada
b) France
c) England
d) Spain

10. The Buffalo Braves became what NBA team?

a) Indiana Pacers
b) Milwaukee Bucks
c) Utah Jazz
d) L.A. Clippers

The NFL Deflategate controversy stemmed from an allegation that, at the 2015 AFC Championship Game, a New England Patriots locker room attendant suspiciously underinflated footballs in a bathroom at what stadium?

Gillette Stadium

11. The movie *61** was filmed in 2001 in this stadium, two years after the last Major League Baseball game had been played in it.

a) Yankee Stadium
b) Cleveland Municipal Stadium
c) County Stadium
d) Tiger Stadium

12. In 1989, who became the first tennis player to host *Saturday Night Live*?

a) Jimmy Connors
b) Chris Evert
c) John McEnroe
d) Billie Jean King

13. Who did the Seattle Pilots become?

a) Seattle Mariners
b) Milwaukee Brewers
c) Kansas City Royals
d) Montreal Expos

In some way, Jerome (Bettis) has touched every person on this team.

-Hines Ward

I don't know, man, I guess
I'm gonna fade into Bolivian.

*-Mike Tyson, when asked what he was going to
do after his fight against Lennox Lewis*

14. In 1987, New York Giants quarterback Phil Simms took home Super Bowl XXI MVP honors with one of the best performances in Super Bowl history by completing 22 of 25 passes for an 88 percent completion rate. Who was the losing quarterback and what team did the Giants defeat?

a) Boomer Esiason, Cincinnati Bengals
b) John Elway, Denver Broncos
c) Jim Kelly, Buffalo Bills
d) Tony Eason, New England Patriots

15. There are only two current original charter members that began play when the NFL was founded in 1920. One is the Arizona Cardinals, who began as the Chicago Cardinals. The other is:

a) New York Giants
b) Chicago Bears
c) Detroit Lions
d) Baltimore Colts

16. Four players in MLB history have hit a home run before turning 20 and after turning 40-
Ty Cobb, Rusty Staub, Alex Rodriguez and:

a) Gary Sheffield
b) Chipper Jones
c) Al Kaline
d) Hank Aaron

17. What golfer won a record 11 consecutive tournaments in 1945?

a) Arnold Palmer
b) Sam Snead
c) Byron Nelson
d) Bobby Jones

18. Who said, "It doesn't matter whether you win or lose, it's how you play the game"?

a) Red Smith
b) Dick Young
c) Grantland Rice
d) Shirley Povich

We get nose jobs all the time in the NHL, and we don't even have to go to the hospital.

-Brad Park

> The only difference between this and Custer's Last Stand was that Custer didn't have to look at the tape afterward.
>
> *-Terry Crisp, former Lightning coach, after his NHL team lost a game 10-0*

19. Before he became a United States President, what All-American center helped the University of Michigan win multiple national titles in football in the 1930s?

a) Ronald Reagan
b) Gerald Ford
c) Richard Nixon
d) Dwight Eisenhower

20. In the longest game in NFL history, what team beat the Kansas City Chiefs on Christmas Day 1971 in a playoff contest with two overtimes and 82 minutes, 40 seconds of action?

a) Houston Oilers
b) Miami Dolphins
c) Buffalo Bills
d) New England Patriots

21. In 2005, the Cardinals beat the 49ers in the first NFL regular season game held outside of the United States. Where was it played?

a) Mexico City
b) London
c) Toronto
d) Montreal

22. Who are the only brothers in MLB history to throw no-hitters?

a) Dizzy and Paul Dean
b) Jim and Gaylord Perry
c) Joe and Phil Niekro
d) Ken and Bob Forsch

23. Who is Edson Arantes do Nascimento?

a) Eddie Arcaro
b) Pele
c) Edward "Whitey" Ford
d) Nene

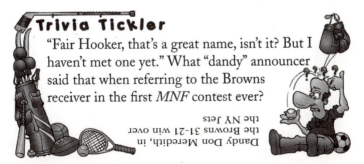

Trivia Tickler

"Fair Hooker, that's a great name, isn't it? But I haven't met one yet." What "dandy" announcer said that when referring to the Browns receiver in the first *MNF* contest ever?

Dandy Don Meredith, in the Browns 31-21 win over the NY Jets

Never have so many spent so much time to sit in relative comfort to brag about their failures.

-Keith Jackson, on golf

24. What "Original Six" team, tied for the longest title drought in the NHL, won their last Stanley Cup in 1967 over the Montreal Canadiens?

a) Toronto Maple Leafs
b) New York Rangers
c) Boston Bruins
d) Chicago Blackhawks

25. Who is the only man to have played for the Braves in Boston, Milwaukee, and Atlanta?

a) Warren Spahn
b) Hank Aaron
c) Eddie Mathews
d) Del Crandall

26. What's the only position not mentioned in Abbott and Costello's *Who's on First?* routine?

a) Shortstop
b) Catcher
c) Right field
d) Left field

27. Two current NFL teams played home games in 1960, their inaugural year, in the Cotton Bowl. One is the Dallas Cowboys. The other is:

a) Houston Texans
b) Kansas City Chiefs
c) Tennessee Titans
d) New Orleans Saints

28. The distance from home plate to second base on a big league diamond is:

a) 120 feet
b) 125 feet, 6.55 inches
c) 127 feet, 3.375 inches
d) 132 feet, 6.755 inches

29. Wilt Chamberlain scored the most points in a single NBA game, 100. Who's second, with 81?

a) Michael Jordan
b) Kobe Bryant
c) Elgin Baylor
d) Rick Barry

I had this great idea to make the Great Wall of China a handball court.

-*George Gobel*

> I have only one superstition.
> I touch all the bases when I hit a home run.
>
> *-Babe Ruth*

30. Who was the first African-American head coach to win a Super Bowl?

a) Lovie Smith
b) Tony Dungy
c) Mike Tomlin
d) Herm Edwards

31. Who holds the MLB record for stealing home plate in a season (8 times) and for a career (54)?

a) Rickey Henderson
b) Ty Cobb
c) Vince Coleman
d) Lou Brock

The New York Mets play their home games in what neighborhood of Queens, NY?

Flushing

32. Who was a member of the University of Houston's golf team and roommate of future pro Fred Couples before becoming a network TV broadcaster?

a) Jim Nantz
b) Pat Summerall
c) Chris Berman
d) Ernie Johnson

33. In 2015, Super Bowl XLIX saw the Patriots defeat the Seahawks 28-24. It also saw the only ejection in Super Bowl history when what Seattle player was tossed for throwing a closed-hand punch at Rob Gronkowski?

a) Richard Sherman
b) Michael Bennett
c) Bruce Irvin
d) K.J. Wright

If you see a defensive team with dirt and mud on their backs, they've had a bad day.
-*John Madden*

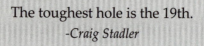

The toughest hole is the 19th.

-Craig Stadler

34. Name the only father-son combination in MLB history to each reach the 50 home run plateau in a single season.

a) Bobby and Barry Bonds
b) Cecil and Prince Fielder
c) Ken Griffey, Sr. and Jr.
d) Yogi and Dale Berra

35. Mickey Mantle is MLB's all-time leader in home runs by a switch-hitter. How many did he hit?

a) 612
b) 536
c) 521
d) 511

36. How many double-stitches are on a baseball?

a) 54
b) 108
c) 216
d) 432

37. What 22-year-old was the youngest player ever to be named the NBA MVP?

a) Derrick Rose
b) Kevin Durant
c) LeBron James
d) Shaquille O'Neal

38. Of the four AFC East teams in the NFL, which one was not an original American Football League franchise?

a) Buffalo Bills
b) Miami Dolphins
c) New England Patriots
d) New York Jets

39. What athlete, while still active, was the winner of Season 14's *Dancing with the Stars*?

a) Kurt Warner
b) Hope Solo
c) Donald Driver
d) Evander Holyfield

Therapy can be a good thing.
It can be therapeutic.
-Alex Rodriguez

> I went to a fight the other night and
> a hockey game broke out.
>
> *-Rodney Dangerfield*

40. In 2012, Augusta National Golf Club invited two women to become its first female members ever. They were:

a) Martina Navratilova and Jennifer Capriati
b) Mia Hamm and Cheryl Miller
c) Bonnie Blair and Jane Fonda
d) Condoleezza Rice and Darla Moore

41. What's the name of the trophy given to the champion of the Canadian Football League?

a) The Blue Cup
b) The Grey Cup
c) The Green Cup
d) The Gold Cup

42. Only one NHL team has won five straight Stanley Cups. Which one?

a) Montreal Canadiens
b) New York Islanders
c) Boston Bruins
d) Chicago Blackhawks

43. In his first two years at Michigan, Tom Brady played backup to what quarterback?

a) Drew Bledsoe
b) Brian Griese
c) Gary Beban
d) Jim Plunkett

44. Who, at 43, was the oldest jockey to ever win horse racing's Triple Crown?

a) Steve Cauthen
b) Eddie Arcaro
c) Willie Shoemaker
d) Victor Espinoza

45. What are the dimensions of a basketball court?

a) 80 feet by 40 feet
b) 86 feet by 44 feet
c) 94 feet by 50 feet
d) 98 feet by 52 feet

Trivia Tickler

What comedian starred in arguably golf's funniest film ever, *Caddyshack*?

Rodney Dangerfield

> I don't talk to kickers.
> What do you say to kickers? "Kick"?
> *-Joe Paterno*

46. Muhammad Ali was heavyweight champion three times during his career. He defeated Sonny Liston in 1964 and George Foreman a decade later. Who did he regain the title from in 1978?

a) Ken Norton
b) Chuck Wepner
c) Joe Frazier
d) Leon Spinks

47. Swimming great Michael Phelps has won an Olympic record 22 total medals. In fact, Phelps has as many gold medals as any other Olympian has regular medals, 18. Who's the Olympian that has 18 total medals?

a) Carl Lewis
b) Larisa Latynina
c) Mark Spitz
d) Jesse Owens

48. Danny Biasone "invented" basketball's
24-second shot clock, which was implemented in:

a) 1984
b) 1974
c) 1964
d) 1954

49. The Yankees have the most World Series
appearances, 40, with a record of 27-13. Who's
second with 20 appearances and an 8-12 mark?

a) Cardinals
b) Giants
c) Dodgers
d) Tigers

50. What movie featured Walter Matthau as the
beer-drinking coach of a Little League team?

a) *Angels in the Outfield*
b) *Rookie of the Year*
c) *Bad News Bears*
d) *A League of Their Own*

As I walked back to the dugout after
striking out, I looked into the stands and
saw my wife and kids booing me.

*-Fran Healy, on when he knew it
was time to call it quits*

> We've all been blessed with
> God-given talents. Mine just happens
> to be beating people up.
> *-Sugar Ray Leonard*

Answers

1. a
2. a
3. b
4. c
5. c
6. b
7. c
8. b
9. a

 This city claims to be the Toilet Paper
Capital of the World and also lays claim
to being the home of the only city-owned
professional sports franchise.

Green Bay, Wisconsin

10. d

11. d

12. b

13. b

14. b

15. b

16. a

17. c

18. c

19. b

20. b

21. a

22. d

23. b

24. a

25. c

26. c

I feel like I'm the best, but you're not
going to get me to say that.
-Jerry Rice

> I feel like a mosquito in a nudist colony.
> I know what to do. I just don't
> know where to start.
> *-Pat Riley, former Heat coach,*
> *on his team's poor record*

27. b

28. c

29. b

30. b

31. b

32. a

33. c

34. b

35. b

36. b

37. a

38. b

39. c

40. d

41. b

42. a

43. b

44. d

45. c

46. d

47. b

48. d

49. b

50. c

Sure the fight was fixed. I fixed it
with my right hand.
-George Foreman

> I have two weapons- my legs,
> my arm and my brains.
> *-Michael Vick*

Teaser Timeout

Touching Base

ymmiJ llasreiP dah a 71-raey gib eugael reerac
dekram yb eno lufroloc tnedicni retfa rehtona. eH
ecno deppets pu ot eht etalp gniraew a seltaeB
giw elihw gniyalp "ria ratiug" no sih tab. rethonA
emit, eh del sreehc rof flesmih ni eht dleiftuo
gnirud skaerb ni yalp. tuB sih erutangis tnemom
emac ni 3691, gniyalp rof eht steM tsniaga eht
seillihP ta eht oloP sdnuorG.

gnicaF aihpledalihP rehctip sallaD neerG, llasreiP
detfol a pop ylf revo eht thgir-dleif ecnef rof sih
ht001 reerac remoh. eugaeL slaiciffo erew ton
desuma ta sih noitarbelec. A yad retal, a gnilur
saw deussi ot tibihorp siht dnik fo roivaheb. fI
ev'uoy daer siht raf, uoy nac ylbaborp sseug tahw
llasreiP did, t'nac uoy?

¡sprɐʍʞɔɐq sǝsɐq ǝɥʇ uɐɹ ǝH

Overtime

Last Laughs

Two runners were trailing the pack in the marathon. The guy who was second-to-last was poking fun at the runner behind him. "Hey, how does it feel to be last?"

"Well, if you must know," said the other guy... And then he dropped out.

Two cannibals were scavenging through a garbage can. One of them came across a discarded *Sports Illustrated* swimsuit issue and said to the other, "Look at this menu!"

Trivia Tickler

Baltimore's first sports statue stands outside Camden Yards, depicting hometown hero Babe Ruth. What's wrong with it?

It shows him wearing a right-hander's mitt. Ruth was a lefty!

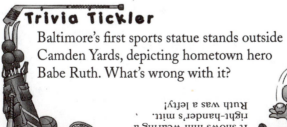

> You know Doc's a nickname, right?
>
> *-Coach Doc Rivers, when asked
> how long one of his players would be
> out with a strained abdominal muscle*

Three guys desperately want to get into the Olympic stadium but the Games are sold out so they decide to pose as athletes. The first guy picks up a long piece of pipe, walks up to the athletes' entrance and says to the guard, "I'm a pole vaulter." The guard lets him in.

The second guy appears with a manhole cover and says, "Discus thrower." He's also allowed in.

The third guy shows up carrying a roll of barbed wire. Confused, the guard looks up and the guy says, "fencing."

Q: Where does a tennis player go for entertainment?

A: Volley-wood

Punch Lines

• A fighter was in the ring with Siamese twins. After the bout he returned home and his wife asked, "Did you win?"

He answered, "Yes and no."

• There was once a boxing referee who worked for NASA. Every time a fighter got knocked down, he'd start counting "10, 9, 8..."

• A good fighter always considers the rights of others.

• The toughest thing about fighting is picking up your teeth with your boxing gloves on.

• And then there was the boxer whose tombstone read, "You can stop counting. I'm not getting up."

My husband is from England and had never seen a football game before. So I could tell him anything I wanted. I told him it was over at halftime.

-Rita Rudner

> Well, Rickey's not one of them,
> so that's 49 percent right there.
>
> *-Rickey Henderson, on reports that*
> *50 percent of ballplayers were using steroids*

Riley says to his psychiatrist, "I'm obsessed with baseball, Doc. It's taken over my life. I eat, drink and think baseball. I even sleep baseball. I dream about it every night. The second I close my eyes I'm running the base paths, fielding a grounder or chasing a fly ball. I wake up more tired than before I went to bed. What can I do, Doc?"

The psychiatrist replies, "The first thing you've got to do is try not to think about the game. For example, when you close your eyes make believe you're watching the lottery results on TV and—wow!—you just won a million dollars!"

"What are you, nuts, Doc?" cries Riley. "I'll miss my turn at bat!"

Before the 1986 Super Bowl between the Chicago Bears and New England Patriots, NBC gave viewers a blank screen to enable them to go to the bathroom. Who won that game?

The Bears, 46-10

A guy was nodding off in his recliner when his wife sneaks up and whacks him on the noggin with a frying pan. Startled, the guy shakes off his cobwebs and says, "What was that for?"

"That was for the piece of paper in your shirt pocket with the name Kelly Ann written on it."

"Aw, shucks," he explains, "a couple of weeks ago when I went to the races, Kelly Ann was one of the horses I bet on."

The wife apologizes for the misunderstanding. A week later, the husband is reading the paper in his favorite chair when she hits him with an even bigger frying pan and knocks him out cold. When he regains his senses, he says, "Geez, what was that for?"

"Your horse called."

Golf is a dumb game. Hitting the ball is the fun part of it, but the fewer times you hit the ball, the more fun you have. Does this make any sense?

-Lou Graham

> I say this from the bottom of my heart,
> that if you don't root for the Dodgers,
> you might not get into Heaven.
> *-Tommy Lasorda*

Little Johnny was in his kindergarten class when the teacher asked the kids what their dads did for a living. The usual jobs came up- fireman, salesman, policeman. Johnny, however, was uncharacteristically shy about giving an answer.

Finally, the teacher said, "Johnny, how about you? What does your father do for a living?"

Johnny murmured, "My dad's an exotic dancer."

The startled teacher quickly ended that segment of class and sent the other kids off to do some coloring. Then she took little Johnny aside and said, "Is that really true about your father?"

"No," said Johnny, "he plays for the Knicks but I was too embarrassed to say it."

Did you hear about the short music afficionado who tried out for the Olympics? He's a compact disc thrower.

Dallas Cowboys owner Jerry Jones, accompanied by some media types, swaggers into an old folks' home to mingle with the people and pick up some good p.r. at the same time. He walks up to a sweet little old lady in a wheelchair who smiles at him with an otherwise blank stare.

"Do you know who I am?" says Jones.

She responds, "No, but if you ask at the desk, they'll tell you."

Boxer: Doc, I can't get to sleep at night.

Doctor: Have you tried counting sheep?

Boxer: It doesn't work. Every time I get to nine I stand up.

A couple in Corpus Christi, Texas, named their son "ESPN" after the sports channel. The parents said the boy is okay with his name, but he's very jealous of his baby brother, "ESPN2."

-Conan O'Brien

> Don't say I don't get along with my teammates. I just don't get along with some of the guys on the team.
>
> *-Terrell Owens*

A husband and wife, both golf fanatics, were discussing the future as they sat by a warm fireplace. "Dear," the wife said, "if I died, would you remarry?"

The husband responded, "Well, if something were to happen to you in the near future, I guess so. After all, we're not exactly senior citizens."

"Would you live in this house with her?" the wife asked.

"I would think so."

She continued, "How about my car? Would she get that?"

"I don't see why not."

"What about my golf clubs? Would you give them to her too?"

"Of course, not!" the husband exclaimed. "She's left-handed."

The punch drunk fighter was nearly killed in a horse riding mishap. He fell from the horse and was almost trampled to death. Fortunately, the Kmart manager came out and unplugged it.

Q: What did the Siamese twins request at the golf club?

A: Tee for two.

"Doctor, we've got an emergency! My baby just swallowed all my golf tees!"

"I'll be there at once."

"What should I do 'til you get here, Doc?"

"Practice your putting."

Trivia Tickler

What "Spaceman" once asked his bosses on the Expos (now Nationals) if he could wear #337 so fans could read his name if he stood on his head?

Bill Lee (LEE)

> I don't think anywhere is there a symbiotic relationship between caddie and player like there is in golf.
>
> *-Johnny Miller*

A Jets fan, Giants fan and Cowboys fan traveled to Saudi Arabia, where they shared a smuggled case of vodka, an illegal activity punishable by death! The Saudi police got wind of the offense and arrested them. Fortunately, the fans had some very good lawyers and were able to reduce the ultimate punishment to life in prison.

As luck would have it, on the day their trial ended, it was the birthday of the Sheik's wife, a Saudi national holiday. The Sheik was feeling particularly benevolent on this celebratory occasion so he decided that the fans could be set free after each of them had received only a whip lashing. In honor of his wife's birthday, the Sheik further declared, "I am going to allow you each one wish before your whipping is administered."

The Jets fan thought quickly and said, "I would like a pillow tied behind my back." His wish was granted and made the whiplashing practically painless.

Next up was the Giants fan. For his single wish,
he asked that two pillows be tied behind his back.
That said and done, his lashing was barely felt.

Finally, it was the Cowboy fan's turn to be
whipped. "And what is your one wish before
you receive your thrashing?" the Sheik asked the
Cowboys fan.

"Please tie the Giants fan to my back."

Q: Why did the racehorse sneak behind the tree?

A: To change his jockeys

Q: What do the Los Angeles Lakers and possums
have in common?

A: Both play dead at home and get killed on the
road.

When I was a kid in Houston, we were so
poor we couldn't afford the last two letters,
so we called ourselves po'.

-George Foreman

> Whatever happened in the past,
> hopefully it's over.
> *-Donovan McNabb*

Q: How many 76ers does it take to change a flat tire?

A: One, unless it's a blowout...Then the whole team shows up.

Q: How many New York Jets does it take to screw in a light bulb?

A: One, and the other ten to recover the fumble

Maybe you've heard about the farmer who crossed his bookie with a hen...He got a chicken that laid odds.

Circle your calendar- November 19th is World Toilet Day. It also marks the day in 1983 when this center scored his 30,000th point, the second in NBA history to do so, behind Wilt Chamberlain. Who is he?

Kareem Abdul-Jabbar, the NBA's all-time leading scorer

Four old duffers had a Saturday morning 8 o'clock tee time for years. On one such morning, they noticed a guy watching them as they teed off. At every tee, he caught up with them and had to wait.

When they reached the fifth tee, the guy walked up to the foursome and handed them a card which read, "I am deaf and mute. May I play through?"

The old duffers were outraged and signaled to him that nobody plays through their group. He'd just have to bide his time.

On the eighth hole, one of the foursome was on the fairway lining up his second shot. All of the sudden he got bopped in the back of the head by the stinging force of a golf ball. He turned around and looked back at the tee angrily.

There stood the deaf mute, frantically waving his arm in the air, holding up four fingers.

Now that I'm retired, I want to say that all defensive linemen are sissies.
    -Former quarterback Dan Fouts

> No, you know. Not at all.
> I don't think so. Some days.
> *-Serena Williams, when asked if*
> *media questions annoyed her*

Q: Where did they put the matador who joined the baseball club?

A: In the bullpen

A female skier was halfway down the slope when she had to go to the bathroom. With no facilities nearby, she found a sheltered area, dropped her pants and bent down. Suddenly she began to slide backwards, then out into the open and down the slope with her pants around her knees. She crashed and broke her leg.

The woman was rushed to the local hospital by ambulance. When the doctor walked into her room, he was laughing hysterically. He said to her, "You're not gonna believe this, but the fellow in the next room said he fell off a ski lift and broke his arm because he saw a naked lady skiing backwards down the mountain. So, tell me... what happened to you?"

Q: What do you get when you cross LeBron James and a groundhog?

A: Six more weeks of basketball

A Braves fan, Cubs fan, Yankees fan and Red Sox fan went rock climbing one day. All the way up the mountain, they were arguing about who was the most die-hard fan.

When they reached the top, the Atlanta fan jumped off the mountain in sacrifice, yelling, "This is for the Braves...Geronimo-o-o-o!"

Not to be outdone, the Chicago fan, in honor of the late great Cubs broadcaster, committed a "Harry Caray" as he too made the ultimate leap of faithfulness from the mountaintop.

Without a flinch, the staunch Yankee backer shouted, "The curse of the Bambino is back!" and pushed the Red Sox fan off the mountain.

I knew it was going to be a long season when, on Opening Day during the national anthem, one of my players turns to me and says, "Every time I hear that song, I have a bad game."

-Former manager Jim Leyland

American Pharaoh has signed a deal with Monster, the energy drink, worth over $7 million. How did he sign the deal?

-Seth Meyers, on the Triple Crown winning horse

A clerk working part-time in a grocery store was having a difficult time with a customer who kept insisting on buying only half a head of lettuce. Finally, the employee went to his manager and said, "Boss, there's some idiot in the produce department who wants only a half a head of lettuce."

Then, out of the corner of his eye he saw the customer standing directly behind him so he quick-wittedly said, "And this gentleman would like to buy the other half."

After the customer was satisfactorily taken care of, the manager praised the clerk for his quick-thinking and asked, "Where are you from?"

He replied, "From Montreal, the city of hockey players and loose women."

The manager shouted, "Hey, my wife's from Montreal!"

"Which team?" said the clerk.

After New England Patriots owner Robert Kraft dies and goes to heaven, God is taking him on a tour of the place. He shows Kraft a small three-bedroom home with a tiny Patriots pennant hanging over the front porch. "This is your eternal home, Robert," says God. "You should feel mighty proud because most folks don't get their own private living quarters here."

Kraft looks at the home, then does an about face and sees this huge four-story mansion with two gigantic Oakland Raiders flags flying between the four marble pillars. And parked in the circular driveway is a black and silver limo with the Raiders logo on the hood.

"Thanks for my home, God," says Kraft, "but I have just one question. You give me this tiny home with a miniature Patriots pennant and Al Davis gets that beautiful mansion. How come?"

God laughs and says, "Oh, that's not Al's home. That's mine."

Trivia Tickler

By what unflattering nickname is the last pick in the NFL Draft commonly known?

Mr. Irrelevant

> Well, I can play in the center,
> on the right, and occasionally on the left.
>
> *-David Beckham, when asked*
> *if he was a volatile player*

A fellow came home from a round of golf and was greeted at the door by his wife dressed in some very alluring attire. "Tie me up," she cooed, "and do anything you want."

So he tied her up and played another round.

Q: How does Floyd Mayweather screw in a light bulb?

A: He holds it up in the air and the world revolves around him.

Q: What do a musical conductor and a baseball statistician have in common?

A: They both know the score.

A Red Sox fan was walking along the beach when a lantern washed ashore. He picked it up and rubbed it. Suddenly a Genie appeared wearing a Derek Jeter jersey. The Genie told the Red Sox fan he had three wishes, but whatever he wished, every single Yankee fan would be granted double that request.

The Boston fan thought long and hard. For his first wish, he asked for a million dollars. Poof! The Sox fan was now a millionaire but, the Genie laughed, every Yankee fan was granted two million dollars.

Then the Red Sox fan wished for a brand new Porsche. Poof! The luxury vehicle magically appeared on the beach as the Genie handed him the keys. The Genie snickered as she explained that every Yankee fan now owned two Porsches.

Now it was time for the Sox fan's third wish and he said, "Listen very carefully, Genie. For my final wish, I want you to choke me half to death."

Statistics are used by baseball fans in much the same way that a drunk leans against a street lamp; it's there more for support than enlightenment.

-Announcer Vin Scully

> Roy Oswalt is a drop and drive pitcher.
> What is a drop and drive pitcher? He is a guy
> who drops and drives. Very simple.
> -*Tim McCarver*

The Cleveland Browns have a brand new cologne
on the market. It has a slightly different twist. You
wear it and the other guy scores.

A golf club walks into a bar. The bartender says,
"Sorry, I can't serve you."

The golf club says, "Why?"

"Because you're going to be driving."

This stadium plays host to numerous
sports events, including NFL games,
and has more toilets- 2,618 -than any
other venue in the world. Name it.

Wembley Stadium, in London